TAKE HEED
Take It to God-Vol. 5

Take Heed, Vol. 5
Take It to God
Copyright © 2022 by Austin Campo

All rights reserved. No part of this book may be reproduced or transmitted in any form or by any means without written permission from the publisher and author.

Additional copies may be ordered from the publisher for educational, business, promotional or premium use.
For information, contact ALIVE Book Publishing at:
alivebookpublishing.com, or call (925) 837-7303.

Book Cover and Interior design by Alex P. Johnson

ISBN 13
978-1-63132-185-6

Library of Congress Cataloging-in-Publication Data
is available upon request.

First Edition

Published in the United States of America by ALIVE Book Publishing
an imprint of Advanced Publishing LLC
3200 A Danville Blvd., Suite 204, Alamo, California 94507
alivebookpublishing.com

PRINTED IN THE UNITED STATES OF AMERICA

10 9 8 7 6 5 4 3 2 1

TAKE HEED

Take It to God-Vol. 5

Austin Campo

ABOOKS
Alive Book Publishing

Dedicated to Cheryl M.

I'm so thankful that God
gave me someone
to hold up my arms
when I just *could not,*
Who tirelessly
prayed and kept
me covered.
I *know* your ear *is* His!

FOREWORD

God has been cleansing and readying a people to assist in bringing in a great end-time harvest of people that don't know Him yet. However, many, even *"in the church,"* have been at best distracted, or worse having given way to money, status, or things. In the end, they all burn anyway. Now, unless they **repent**, they will not take part helping Him while He shows Himself real to many *worldwide*.

Simultaneously, great changes in the way we operate in this world, natural disasters, wars, economic hardship, and divisive tactics through people with agendas will all happen, *as usual*. The ebb and flow that has existed since the beginning after sin entered, continues, and escalates. Meanwhile, in the spirit, the war between good and evil rages.

Please just be warned. God is a good God, but He is also serious. He is *holy*. For those that already believe, there is *no time* to not have time for Him, or to push off those things that He wants you to do, or not do.

Yesterday I was given *"I AM is very weary with elevating people and then they take **the lost** out of their daily to-do list."*

Then today the word I was to read was Obadiah. He paralleled to me *three sets* of *verses* to my country, America, while *I "saw"* people all *going under water*. Then I was given this message: *"All should take stock of where they are personally, because America is going under. They love money more than the God that held them above the boundaries, as an example to the world, of the FAVOR of **the GOD**."* So please, *take heed*.

CHAPTER ONE

The Bird Cage
Received

Pentecost Sunday was June 5, 2022, which was 8 days after having a major surgery. Six days after Pentecost, the ministering angels told me I had been in a *testing period*. This was kind-of a relief, because it had been consistently hard to *"see"* in the spirit, and overall, just a lot of spiritual warfare, at a time I was also physically depleted.

Instead of asking *how I did*, I asked what day I was on. *I saw* a "6". I thought, "Oh." So, then I asked what time the testing would be over the next day. The answer came, simply, not long after I went to bed, *"Tomorrow."* The next thing I remember, I was waking up.

In the same spot of my kitchen that I often talk to the Lord in the morning, I was surprised when the angels excitedly told me that I passed my tests. They spelled it out. Then I was excited too, and relieved. The last time I was told I had finished a testing period, they described that I'd made it "one step away" from the top of whatever the test was. That time, in my mind, I saw a staircase and saw the next step and the upper landing. I was disappointed in myself, and already wondering what it was I didn't complete or get right. However, the angels reassured me that time. So, I felt pretty good having passed this time considering I had been through a lot and was still recovering.

Then they told me I was now at *a gate*. I asked a short series of questions, all basically trying to find out what kind of gate it was, and what would happen when I walked through. As I said in a previous book, I am a "question-girl," that's how I process.

On an unknown date I saw what looked like a *bird cage* moving, but it had a person in it. I didn't get it at that point, though I soon would. I thought the enemy was trying to put me in a cage, and was just trying to interrupt the flow of my spiritual sight.

In reality, *the angels* were telling me I was going into a cage, and though I don't see continuous visions in color much anymore, they showed it as very beautiful, and golden. Had I realized that *they were telling me* I would be in a cage, I might have just stopped everything. I was just so exhausted and felt like everything was becoming too hard.

Poised to write this book, honestly, I was disheveled anyway. I was early in the midst of trying to recover from the surgery and still using a walker when I apparently went into this *"bird cage"* phase. Then, I had the first of two bad medication reactions.

I wasn't one to take a lot of meds. I took vitamins. Years before I quit taking meds because the doctor back then and I were worried about them damaging my organs. So, I didn't take anything unless I absolutely had to, and I built a very high pain tolerance.

The medication they gave me was a very strong one. Despite not wanting to be on a narcotic even temporarily,

Chapter 1

I *seemed* to be doing okay at first. After I, *unknowingly*, entered the bird cage. I was not only exhausted, I started getting some anxiety. Specifically, I had feelings of growing insecurity. By then I was probably half a week in, both thinking and saying, "Wow, Lord, why so much warfare *now*?" He didn't really answer. So, I kept persevering best I could, but I was now *dreading* nighttime, during which I was constantly having my husband, my family members, the books, my job, provision, *everything*, threatened! It was like the enemy almost *completely* took over my spiritual sight. Try as I might, it was like the angels weren't helping me much and I didn't understand why. So, then I felt a bit abandoned, like I was alone, even though I knew at the same time, *they **were** there*. I would seem to break through for a minute or two just to get lambasted again.

This went on and on, until the climactic conclusion came, being one night that was fiercely made everything about *me*! The demonic realm came at me so strong, just one thing after another, after another. They harped on things I'd done wrong, and stomped on *every* fear or insecurity that had ever been an issue. Even though I knew I had repented (turned away from), and am forgiven of everything, the constant battering was wearying my heart and tearing at my peace. They were relentless!

It was coming so fast and hard I could barely keep up, let alone deal with each thing. I was threatened. I was shown I had cancer. They kept showing me that I'd be in a wheelchair, or I was going to get hit by a semi on my trike, etc.

Sometimes I kept my wherewithal to fight back. I would call their bluff, basically, loose them from me, and bind them as they would be in heaven, and send them packing. However, sometimes I just laid there, trying ***not to see*** at all. That never worked though, because when I'm awake I can always ***"see,"*** with my eyes closed. I couldn't get away from it all!

Toward the end, *I felt* at daybreak it was all over for me. Something awful would happen and I'd be taken away, or die. Then right at the end, just as the sun was starting to come up, I heard a very angry voice saying, "I don't care! Shoot down through the window if you have to!" I just laid there and said something like, "Lord, I don't know what's about to happen but please just take care of my family."

Then, silence. The sun was now shining. My belly was gripped, but I went to the windows and peeked around a side of a curtain to peer out. There was nothing there. No man, no woman, *no demons* bounding around me. Whoosh, just like that, it went from *chaos* and *terror* to *calm*, and *peace*.

At that moment I knew whatever all that was, it was over. Right after I thought, "What is that med again?!" So, I went and got the bottle, and realized it was a generic of a pill I could not take about 22 years before. I *never* took another one.

A day and a half later I was prescribed another narcotic. For three weeks or so it seemed to be okay. Then I broke out in a two-tiered rash.

In my case, the bird cage period seemed to be in stages. First, I was just trapped. This included my waking life as well, as I could not drive and was not able to do much. At night, I was dealing with warfare and trying to stay comfortable at the same time.

It was humbling having to have a toilet with grip bars

Chapter 1

over the regular one, and have a bath seat in the shower, with my husband helping me in and out.

I saw the bird cage again July 27th. It was as if I was seeing from inside it, out. I saw the door just go up, as if by invisible hands. Then I was getting around better and feeling better, with a little more freedom, being taken out from time to time, etc. Still, just all the little details were awry. The rash took quite a while to leave. I itched and hurt.

Things were progressing, however my foot did not come all the way back after surgery. Some parts I could not feel at all, others parts had feeling but was hyper-exaggerated. It felt like some toes were tethered, as if I had a very tight ace bandage over part of it, and it I had a "bunchy" feeling under that foot. (Much of that is still the case)

I was doing some work from home and didn't feel comfortable to go back at first. Then did 3 days for a while after that. The foot has been a problem driving but I have managed. It does still set the leg off and I start having muscle spasms. It has been just an odd, hard reset.

Around that time, I saw the bird cage again, empty. Unless I am forgetting a time, I believe that is also when I then saw a group of people walking into the cage and looking around and then exiting. When I asked what it meant I was told I was out of the birdcage. That date as 9/15/2022. My friend, Cheryl, said it was exactly 50 days after being in the cage looking out. Since that time my bp and pulse have gone a little crazy. Let's just say that this lady, who rarely went to the doctor has been to *many*, often. It has been a hard, *exhausting* period.

The spiritual warfare, does continue, but eventually got

back to more what I normally experience when writing the series' books.

God does not tempt us. However, sometimes we leave *"spiritual doors"* open through sin; or God allows the *enemy* simply try to take us out one way or another.

Proverbs 17:3 says, *"The refining pot is for silver and the furnace for gold. But* **the Lord tests hearts.***"*

Just so I make sure you understand, the first medication certainly did have a part in what happened, but do not think for a minute it was all the drug. There truly is a God and a devil. There truly is someone who took the penalty for all of us, so we could be reconciled to God and go to heaven one day. His name is *Jesus*. There truly are angels and demons. The enemy hates believers and does all kinds of things to try to keep anyone away from God. Be aware. *Take heed.*

CHAPTER TWO

It was early morning. Without an introduction, I had an interactive vision. That's how I describe having a vision and the Lord using other senses, like hearing, feeling, or smelling during. The vision follows.

The Window is Closing
August 22, 2022

I saw a woman's figure dressed as the heavenly hosts do, standing near a stream. A thought crossed my mind that she was me. The stream was flowing toward my view. Then I realized there were crowds of people on both sides of the stream that continued flowing through.

Suddenly, the woman's figure stepped with one foot all the way across. She was now shown straddling over the water flowing, with one foot on each side. At that moment, again, I thought it was me. As I had that thought this time though, I felt as if I was being disciplined. I had the feeling first, but then I had a couple thoughts follow right behind. First, I thought of how I made things the prior weekend more important than God and His book. So, immediately, I repented of it, meaning in my heart I resolved to turn from that. I stated what I felt I'd done wrong and I asked for forgiveness. Then, thoughts of the busyness of life and how often in the last months I allowed so many things to distract me and take priority over Him. I then repented again, knowing I had done this. I quickly asked Him for forgiveness. Then, I no longer felt His discipline.

I saw the woman's figure again and I said, with emphatic words, something like, "No! Don't let me straddle between You and the world!" and immediately I saw the foot left on the original side come off and over to the other side. Still, I saw the woman's figure with now both feet *precariously* trying to balance right on the edge of the water! I also saw that the stream was now *higher, wider* and running *fuller* and *faster* between both sides. It no longer looked like a stream, but a river!

I said something like, "No Lord, don't let me stand on just the edge! Let my feet both be planted firmly on Your side!" As I looked again, the figure was not only away from the edge, but seated, and so were all the others on that side. That was the end of the vision.

The vision was for me. However, it is a word for *all of us*, all His "church", His people, as a whole.

He showed me I was a bit on both sides. He also was saying, many are straddling both sides. He used me to be corrected and led me to state it here, so that He could speak to you if you need to repent as well. It was for *all of us*.

I was reminded of a window I'd "seen" closing many times for a while, before this particular day. I mistakenly thought it was about the time to write this book was closing. However, He was telling me that the window *for His church to repent*, is coming to a close. It was both a plea and a warning to make sure you are where you need to be. Take heed!

Chapter 2

Pecans and People
October 23, 2022

At our home we have two mature pecan trees. This year they were more loaded than ever before. We found out the hard way a couple years ago, that you not only have to be diligent to go out and collect them as they drop to the ground, but you have to guard what you collected. After a 5-gallon bucket was collected, it was set inside my husband's building. What was not considered, is that the chipmunks can make themselves extremely small, and still get in. Little by little the chipmunks took them away, until pretty much the whole harvest was taken. As it was happening, we thought friends and family had simply let themselves in and taken some, as they were told they could. In reality, it all went nut by nut by small animals while we had the ability to stop that from happening.

Today I went out with the dogs and collected the nuts. Very soon after I started this, I knew the Lord was talking to me through the Holy Spirit and likely the angels.

Though my husband cleaned up and mowed down the area to make it easy to collect the nuts as they fall, the wind was crazy for a couple days, so small branches and twigs, nut hulls, with nuts and without, were all over the area. To further block me seeing the good nuts, mixed in there were nuts with an end bit off or half a nut just gone. The chipmunks already had dined out at the bottom, just as the blue jays were getting take-out up top.

As I continued going through the area back and forth, I was made to think of the difference of the nuts. Along with the beautiful new nuts, freshly dropped, there were also some good nuts that had come down with their hull on, both closed and split. Others that came down, again, from last year, nut and hull were both dark brown and hard. They basically died in there before they were born.

Then I was led to think about myself in the Lord's place and these pecans as people. The pecans were in all states, so are the people that do not know Him yet and also *those that do*.

There were some that were dried up, whose shells had become hard, even brittle. These are ones that endured hard things, sometimes broken beyond what our human mind fathoms, sometimes even broken in pieces.

It is also some that knew Jesus but were hurt, some, even in church. An anger or even hurt was constructed much like the hull to protect their heart or even their pride.

Some were simply stuck in one spot, and they represented people that had that "just one thing" holding them back from being free. These are the ones that came to Jesus and later fell away, or the ones that just have that *"one more thing"* **they** have to change to come to Jesus at all. Others were in a hull that just fell but the nut was peeking out and the outside was still pliable to remove the pecan. These are those that may have the world's coat on, but are open and ready to receive a real and loving Christ.

We had failed to make sure the nuts were safe. Once we had them, we simply went on and continued with everything else. Even as we saw they were disappearing, we chalked it up to something happening that wasn't. One by one, they disappeared. This is what happens when those that already believe show little to no love to the ones that *Jesus just made His own*. They are new to faith, they are new to belief, they are new in a church or whatever the setting, and likely don't know much about it all. They just have the important thing, *HIM*. When we fail to encourage, we don't have time for questions, often times they don't just walk away from whatever setting they found him. Often, they long for something they're connected to or is familiar. Often newly faithed people walk away from Him too.

They, all of them, are people that God wants to reach. Some might have known Jesus and just were taken by hurt, bitterness, the cares of this life, addiction, heartbreak, betrayal, and any other number of things. Others, have never known Him at all. What they all have in common, is HE is the answer.

I was shown a parallel so I could understand the correlation. Jesus is the good shepherd. He is the Way, Truth and the life. Every single issue they are dealing with, or not dealing with, He loves them right where they are. Just as I was harvesting for my home, a great harvest will happen so He can invite them to be His own. Walking out of the area today, I knew that He expects *us* to love them all enough, to help Holy Spirit bring them in. Luke 15: 3-7 NKJV is a parable that says: *"So He spoke this parable to them, saying: "What man of you, having a hundred sheep, if he loses one of them, does not leave the ninety-nine in the wilderness, and go after the one which is lost until he finds it? And when he has found it, he lays it on his shoulders, rejoicing. And when he comes home, he calls together his friends and neighbors, saying to them, 'Rejoice with me, for I have found my sheep which was lost!' I say to you that likewise there will be more joy in heaven over one sinner who repents than over ninety-nine just persons who need no repentance."*

CHAPTER THREE

Discord and Death
Received: September 9/20/22

I asked that a word would bubble up in me. I didn't necessarily ask that it be for the book, but this word came quickly and clear. It follows.

"Many national leaders will rise and fall quickly. Some, even newly elected, will lose their seats. A large voice, a "wind" from the east, a political wind, comes that allows Soros to divide Latin voters' districts.

It will be a time of great division, a total anti-government time at a very volatile place. A Boston tea party leader is assassinated, and a William and Mary University is taken by force. Many are executed."

Received 10/1/2022

I received a bit of additional information. It follows.

"Radical right at Virginia will arrest left. It turns violent. Eventually the right who carried this out is apprehended. However, this causes the Virginia Governor to enact martial law."

A Time to Prepare
August 2022 (unknown date)

In a way the next part seems backwards, but it is the order I received it. It is simply a short list of ways to prepare for the time we are getting ready to experience. It does not cover everything for long-term. It is to be ready for a particular time, which will follow.

A day in August of 2022 I received the following.

"Have extra ammo. Have your guns at an arm's length or closer. Team up with others. (General thoughts ran through my mind about one having food, another having water, and other things) *Date your cans 8 months beyond the expiration dates. If there are no expiration dates, you can weigh and mark the weight on each. Then if you are not sure if something is good, weigh again. What happens is that you lose volume and it weighs less after it goes bad."*

An American Bird Cage
August 2022 (unknown date)

It made sense that I experienced a *"bird cage"* beforehand because the angels would use the term again when we moved into this time. Something happens in the U.S. and martial law is imposed. For two weeks everyone will be home and *will not go anywhere*. It will take an *emergency* to go *anywhere* at the time.

By five weeks after the event, everyone will need I.D. to travel anywhere *within* the United States, *and inspections are imminent.*

When I realized that it talked about martial law, I asked if it should be connected to what was already given concerning William & Mary but was told it is two separate events.

A Watch Team
Received 4/26/2022

D.E., who buys books and reads, is a top aide to A.E. of the Treasury Department. (Names purposely withheld) She read "Take Heed Vol. 4–*A Time of Persecution.*" After, she spoke to A. E., who also reads, about some of the contents. E. sometimes also talks to a top agent at the F.B.I. After he read the parts in question, he told the agent about it, explaining *"A Titanic Takeover"* from chapter 4 of that book, which involved England and France.

To Be Honest
Received 10/16/2022

To be honest, I did not want to post names I received on "A Watch Team." Instead, I asked if I could just do initials. One, these things have not happened yet. Two, I wasn't sure I had one of the last names correct. Also, there are people on the other side of this equation who have no idea I now have received this information! As far as I can tell, *they were concerned* in the first place.

I was told I could use initials. So, I asked to do a different word than one listed on a word I felt could also cause issues. The angels *immediately* showed me the first letter of the word **boldly**. At the same time, I *felt* corrected. So, I surrendered that God wanted the word in, not changed.

Here I am again. The following is yet one more thing that I did not have until today, that includes some things I was concerned about *again*. A thought about a few *what ifs*, like being sued or imprisoned crossed my mind. I'm just one woman who sees and hears things. People in high places can make things seem like whatever they want. So, I asked again, despite what happened last time, if we really wanted to do as-is.

This time I saw angels and they *were not happy!* I saw one angel go briskly and take my view back to the large birdcage that I was in before. I basically pleaded, not to be trapped with the enemy able to come at me that way again. I was then surrendering in heart and speech, but the same angel left and came back quickly with a clothes hanger in his hand. He started moving his mouth and waving the hanger around. I could not hear his voice but his face looked angry. I've never seen one look quite like that. Inside, I immediately just *knew* he was saying, "Have I ever left you hanging?!" So, I surrendered again. Then I finished the *"Threading the Needle,"* and thought that was it.

The scripture given for this chapter is Daniel 4:8 NKJV. *"I saw the ram pushing westward, northward, and southward, so that no animal could withstand him; nor was there any that could deliver from his hand, but he did according to **his will** and became great.*

CHAPTER FOUR

Threading the Needle
Received: 10/16/2022

Before I relay the vision given, when I asked what I was to name this part, I was shown 2 different ways of someone threading a needle, then just given the words. I had no idea what it meant outside of actually getting thread through the eye of the needle. However, Wiktionary at https://en.wiktionary.org/wiki/thread_the_needle#:~:text=(idiomatic) says it is: *"To find harmony or strike a balance between conflicting forces, interests, etc."*

Additionally, for new readers, both *"Threading the Needle"* and *"A Watch Team"* of this volume are part of the same event, already in Take Heed-A Time of Persecution-Vol. 4, called *"A Titanic Takeover."*

Setting: I was up early and was praising God a bit with *Church International* playing on my t.v. I moved to refill coffee or something and landed standing in the place of my kitchen where I often talk to God in the morning. I saw a lot of white moving. Looking intently, I saw heavenly Host coming up from the lower level, coming around where the stairs go up, just everywhere. Then I saw a capital "I" come toward me and then pause and keep moving. The "I" looked the same as when the angels spell out "**I AM**" to me. It appears as, wide, cloud-like letters. My eyes were drawn to it and I saw it move over to where my chair is in the living area. So, I went to sit down. Then the vision started.

Vision

I saw D.C. As I started to ask about D.C., I saw a ship slowly passing by me. Then the scene changed.

Then I saw a "game" table, sitting in a big venue. It appeared green with one black stripe showing vertically from my sight. I did not look away, but then there was the model of a ship sitting, also vertically, in the center of the table.

Then I watched as I saw two sets of legs and feet walk up to either side at the NW and NE corners of the table. I could see they were wearing suits. After, a hand and arm came in from the person at the right corner and it threw a big chunk of money on the table.

Interpretation

It is a game, a *threading the needle*, as stated above. The ship sitting in the middle is, unfortunately, a pawn being used in the "game". Two nations come to terms, one from the western hemisphere and one from the eastern hemisphere. This was shown by the positioning of the stripe on the table, the two walking from left and right, with the ship and table portrayed vertically.

The one from the eastern hemisphere throws a considerable amount of money to the one from the western hemisphere to "come to agreeable terms" with whatever their part of the deal is.

At this point *I felt* God was **angry**! For a second I thought I did something, but then the message came.

Message to Me
Words & Vision

"Tell them in the book, the window is closing to exercise a war that is steam-rolling a tanker and the I.U.!" I asked about I.U. but then *just knew* it had something to do with shipping, therefore, "international units". Then came the following, through words and vision.

Staged

E. transported I.U. to Ukraine, a part they lie about. (I saw as if someone was running up a vertebra like stairs) There is a hidden agenda to claim the shipping lanes to control the *takeover*, (previously mentioned in volume 4) and to plant a flag on France. They want the whole *"leg and foot"*. As this was stated I saw what almost looked like the Lunar landing, with someone actually forcibly shoving a flagpole with flag in the dirt.

The scene panned out, and I saw the territory moving and the name changing on the map.

Then I saw a ***stage***. I saw at first from high up. The place was huge and it was packed. It had beautiful maroon layers of curtains, with gold tie-backs and a topper on top. It was as if I was viewing a *grand theater*.

Then my view was from much closer but still above a bit. My eyes were drawn to the stage, which at first seemed like it had a big insignia, like a huge signet or watermark on it. Then I realized it was digital, beause I saw the world rotating, and an image of live people holding hands rotating around it.

Then I saw six people come out as if they were really excited. They were all holding hands, and came to the front and took a grand bow. I could not see who they were, but I do know the audience erupted with what looked like frenzied clapping, standing, etc.

Interpretation

When the goals are achieved, it later somehow all becomes part of a *world agenda*. Initiatives, laws, the way the world works will change, and the event outlined was just a cog or piece of the greater planned agenda. This was shown with the large digital world rotating and the people shown of all nationalities rotating around it.

Some of the key players will be exalted like royalty or rock stars by people everywhere, furthering them to more easily reach their objectives.

There are **six nations** *strongly* involved in this. This is shown with six people coming out excitedly, and bowing because they were excited about the achievement and receiving great applause and ovation from all the people.

It has all been *staged*. The people who gain adoration and even fame in this, are like actors on a stage. Most of the people fall for all of it, and believe what they've seen and been told. (End of vision/word)

Today I asked what scripture, I was supposed to read, immediately I was given: **Jeremiah 22, 23**, and **24**. Before I'd even read all, I asked the Lord, "Why 22?" Then He answered: *"America was a nation that asked to abound more* *than any had seen at that time. America now is a nation that wants a tryst with a tyrant, who makes an evil covenant and will slit America's throat."*

CHAPTER FIVE

Received 2/2/2022

The harvest Jesus was promised is full and getting ready to be ushered into the kingdom. If we believe but are still wallowing in sin, doing things, we know we shouldn't, or just living distracted from the One who gave us *life* and *freedom*, then we render ourselves useless or ineffective for the work He has for us. If that's where we are, without **true** *repentance*, then even if we witness the greatest revival ever seen, we will see it as a ***witness***, and not His ***worker***.

God is serious! Trials, tribulations and *the Tribulation* is coming. Things will happen never seen before. The world will keep spinning, cataclysmic things will happen, yet people will go on, as if nothing is a big deal. Simultaneously, God will also be leading people here and there through the Holy Spirit, and they will be helping to "bring in" those who do not know Him yet, *but will*.

If you already believe, just go before Him and make *sure* you are ready. If you do not know Him, this is a great time to come to know the hope *Jesus* brings you, the love He brings you, and the way He's made for you to be reconciled to our Creator.

As stated before, for those who say they are His already, the window to be cleansed, prepared, ready, is closing.

Repent therefore, if you need to!

Do it now! Do not wait! We are never promised another day. We *think* we're doing okay, and sometimes think, *"Well, I'm already clean,"* or *"God knows my heart."* Yes, yes, He does, but sometimes our flesh lies, or the demons do. The Word says: *"The heart is deceitful above all things, And desperately wicked; Who can know it?"* NKJV

When in Rome
Received 6/16/2022

In three days (6/19/2022), the Vatican will talk with a *tyrant*, a **D.S.** (name seemed Slavic) however, was not clear and leaving un-named). Allies Wotad, and a "Hue" takes a helicopter to watch the exchange.

Interpretation

I have no real interpretation of it, or the players. The person or people at the Vatican were not named. I got a name for the tyrant, but I am not sure the spelling. I did look up "Wotad," and two things popped up repeatedly: World of Tanks, a MMO online tank battle game, that popped up as videos or game icons, and an acronym for *"The worship of the all mighty dollar."* Found at https://www.urbandictionary.com/define.php?term=wotad.

Guns
Received 6/23/2022 – undated

I saw assault weapons, floating by, upright, just the guns.

Then I saw inside what looked like a school hallway, with lockers. Then both assault weapons *and handguns* were just sort-of floating between me and the lockers I saw. (End of vision)

As there have been so many lives lost in schools across the country, legislators have been trying to get all assault weapons banned. It appears that the House of Representatives passed a ban on assault weapons in August of 2022. However, when I had this vision, it had not taken place as of yet.

Interpretation

People seek to ban assault weapons. As I saw only assault weapons at first, but then saw both assault weapons and handguns. I believe they will seek to ban handguns also, and possibly remove conceal carry and constitutional carry in states that have it all at the same time. (End of interpretation)

As time goes by and the "late" time we are in gets *later*, I *feel* they will move legislation and make it *disarm all the people* that are not in whatever authority is in place at that time. Not all will give up their weapons.

Towers and A Can
Received 10/25/2022

"Radical right threatens cell towers and it opens a can of worms. D.C. rolls out a uniform code that makes threatening a tower **treason**.

*Radical right, here, is not speaking of all "right-leaning" persons. This is referring to people with conservative views who resort to more than peacefully protesting. I felt the Lord wanted me to state this.

Riots and Death
Received 6/23/2022

I saw "Poor Jill," and I asked "Jill who?? Then I saw the White House from a distance. Then it looked and felt I was moving, as my view seemed from much closer. At first, I saw dark things in front of me. At first, I thought they could be bushes. Moving closer still, I realized I was moving that they were protesters, a lot of them.

My gaze seemed to move beyond the crowds to see clearly. I saw people exiting from the White House. It appeared to be near the front but on the right side. They were moving quickly toward vehicles. I was told the secret service took an Eva away, and then it *erupts*. A Pres. Biden admin. uses Lt. D.E. as a shield, and a terrible assassin takes a SRT Assault rifle.

I was shown no more in that vision or who was killed.

I received another prophecy about this on 9/28/2022. The Lord did not want me to relay the details. Instead, the angels said, *"You are a prophet. Declare it is not attempted and that the plot is discovered."* So, that is what I did.

Nothing I am writing in this book is out of my personal political bend. I am writing what I have received from the Lord through the angels, and told to share.

CHAPTER SIX

Internment
Received 8/12/2022

My husband and I went to his friends' cabin in Pennsylvania. This particular day he took me to a place the locals call *"Top of the World."* Out of nowhere I received the following message:

"*I AM is opening a window of time.* (I *saw* a window opening) *An angel will take you to heaven and you will be escorted to see the wounded in the Internment Camp in Atlanta."* So, I asked if an internment camp was what I thought it was, a holding center for prisoners of war. The angel simply said, *"Atlanta is the enemy's acquisition."*

I was **not** taken to heaven that night or any other while there. When I asked what happened, stating I did not remember anything. I was told the following. *"I AM said you can't. Your heart started racing."* Later I asked again. Then I was told, *"You really do love people. Your heart raced and you stopped breathing."* It is true I'd had a major surgery about 6 weeks before. Unbeknownst to me until later, my blood pressure and pulse had started spiking and dropping.

"A Take Heed Event"
Received: August 2022

To preface this one, it appears to be an event that has been threaded through Vol. 3, *The Elijah Anointing,* Vol. 4, *A Time of Persecution,* and now here with more information. It is obvious that He wants you to know what the enemy would do.

I was told the event was going to take place a certain date, but was then told they did not carry out due to a shipment they were using being "dead," Tannerite. I was directed to put it in this book, so I believe there is still a plan. *Take Heed*, and pray!

The Message This Time

"Six terrorists "in" West Virginia will detonate a bomb in South Carolina. It is on a timer (saw a laptop more than once) *and will go off in a tunnel under a train with a lot of passengers. It will be remotely controlled."*

As I said, this is the **third volume** in a row that *this event* has been threaded though. The previous accounts, had different details. It is *obvious* to me we are being **warned** over, and over and now over again.

I asked if they *lived* in West Virginia then go to South Carolina to set the bombs (plural) off. *At that time,* I was told they were in a house in Tennessee, then they would go to South Carolina to set the bombs in the tunnels in *Charleston.* (Obviously that did not happen then, but am relaying it in case they take the same planned route if attempted again.)

To continue, after the event, the water will be radioactive.

I was told it would be the worst event ever to happen to the eastern coast of the U.S.

Please *take heed*, and pray.

The Axis
Received: 7/22/2022

"The earth will move off its axis and three times, time just halts. A dormant earthquake fault-line is waking up." I was told it would be much later. I was not given the fault-line or the time period. There was a lot of warfare immediately after receiving the very short message. However, He wanted it in the book.

I believe this is something that likely takes place very, very late, and likely might have something to do with the next thing I was given. (below)

Mount Ararat
Received: 8/12/2022

"In the tail end. . . lava will flow out of Mt. Ararat." I *saw* what looked like a dam, or sections of one that were varying sizes. I wondered if it was the mountain rock simply protruding out, but it looked more like metal. Then on my second view I saw what looked like a steering wheel on it. Just then it was as if various sections were breaking, and lava was *rushing* through.

I then asked if this event would be at the tail end of the book, or the tail end of the world as we know it. An angel said, *"At the tail end of time."*

Matthew 24: 8 NKJV says: *"Take heed that no one deceives you. For many will come in my name saying, 'I am the Christ,' and will deceive many. And you will hear of wars and rumors of wars. See that you are not troubled; for all these things **must come to pass**, but the end is not yet. For nation will rise against nation, and kingdom against kingdom, and there will be famines, pestilences, and earthquakes in various places. All these are the beginning of sorrows."*

Leaving on A Lot of Cliff Hangers
Today, 10/24/2022

For a while, and really a lot lately, I was trying to get this book done. One, it has been *late*. The Lord extended it at least twice that I can remember. While I had spiritual warfare through *every* volume as I was writing them, I believe it came to a *very harsh* and *tiring pinnacle* for me on *this* volume, because it is *the last*.

With all honesty, and my apology, from barely into writing Take Heed- *"Journeying in the Supernatural"* – Vol. 1, I knew there were to be **7 books**. However, God's original plan was to have *all* the books finished and published quite a while ago now. It had to do with *timing*, and *people that read* and *people who are drawn to the supernatural*, because He *is* a supernatural God. The books were all to be out so there was time for people to see them. His plan was to *seed* into people, to water seeds already in others, and to bring in people that have *never known Him at all* or knew of Him but were not in relationship with Him. **He also wanted to warn us all**.

My time writing this series was both *excruciating* and *fulfilling*. The things I've seen lit up all kinds of emotions but, oddly enough, only after they were written down. Warfare has been exhausting much of the time, and sadly, seems to have aged me 10 years instead of 2. After awhile every physical issue I had also lit up, causing more pain that I'd dealt with up 'til then, and brought on a surgery with rods and screws, a foot that isn't all the way back, and issues with blood pressure which I never had before.

I am convinced that the attacks overnight whether sleeping or awake and always for a time when I woke, truly affected my physical body.

Beyond that, some people *I love* have not even read the books! Others started and could not finish. I am pretty sure some think I've lost my mind or have an extremely vivid imagination. Believe me, the old devil loves to poke me with that. Doing something like this is ***not*** easy.

So why would I say fulfilling? I was asked to do it so people might be helped by the *Holy Spirit*, come to *Jesus Christ*, and be reconciled to their heavenly Father, God. He wanted to reach readers through these little books, so He could reach ***them***. I was just a human component, actively walking out, my call. I was doing what I was asked for this time.

I have certainly done things before, but maybe this time I felt the greatest toll. Still, I felt I was right where I was supposed to be, doing *exactly* what *He wanted*. I have no regrets, except since I took too long, two books *disappeared* out of whatever hands they would have reached, *and* the Library of Heaven. For that I have asked forgiveness.

Mainly, the Lord led me to write this portion, to remind people choosing Him does not mean bad things will not happen. It does not mean you will not have trying times. In fact, the Word clearly states you will. He gives all of us free will. We all have a choice, *to know Him* or not, *choose Him* or not, and *love Him* or not. Please, *take heed* and choose well. Blessings!

"Behold, I stand at the door and knock. If anyone hears My voice and opens the door, I will come in to him and dine with him, and he with Me." Revelation 3:20 **NKJV**

As I always encourage, *please* take anything I have written to the Lord yourself. He wants a relationship with you *personally*. Whether you personally know Jesus yet or not though, I believe Holy Spirit will give you the answer to anything you ask.

God bless you. May you all *take heed* . . . .and *take it to God!*

Sincerely,
Austin Campo

ABOOKS

ALIVE Book Publishing and ALIVE Publishing Group
are imprints of Advanced Publishing LLC,
3200 A Danville Blvd., Suite 204, Alamo, California 94507

Telephone: 925.837.7303
alivebookpublishing.com

www.ingramcontent.com/pod-product-compliance
Lightning Source LLC
Chambersburg PA
CBHW020024050426
42450CB00005B/635